Money Made Simple

An Australian Guide to Building Wealth and Freedom

By Mavis Bloom

Copyright

Money Made Simple: An Australian Guide to Building Wealth and Freedom
Copyright © 2025 Mavis Bloom
All rights reserved.

No part of this publication may be reproduced, stored in a retrieval system, or transmitted in any form or by any means — electronic, mechanical, photocopying, recording, or otherwise — without prior written permission of the author, except for brief quotations used in reviews or scholarly works.

Disclaimer: This book is for educational and informational purposes only. It is not financial, legal, or tax advice. The author is not a licensed financial adviser. Readers should seek independent professional advice before making any financial decisions. The author and publisher disclaim liability for any loss or risk incurred as a result of the use and application of the contents of this book.

ISBN: 978-1-7643098-0-6
Cover design: Mavis Bloom
Printed in Australia / Printed on demand worldwide

Dedication

For every Australian who's ever thought,

"I'll never get ahead"

This book is proof that you can.

Copyright..2
Dedication..3
Introduction - Why This Book Matters Now............6
Chapter 1 - The Aussie Money Trap - And How to Escape It..8
Chapter 2 - The Real Cost of a Latte - Understanding Your Spending..............................12
Chapter 3 - Building Your Money Map - The 3-Account System......................................16
Chapter 4 - The Bare-Bones Budget - Spending Only on What Matters...............................21
Chapter 5 - Automate to Dominate - Setting Your Finances on Autopilot.............................26
Chapter 6 - The Emergency Fund - Your First Financial Safety Net....................................30
Chapter 7 - The Debt Detox Breaking Bad Money Habits...34
Chapter 8 - Good Debt vs. Bad Debt - The Australian Perspective....................................39
Chapter 9 - Smarter Mortgage Management - Owning Your Home Sooner........................44
Chapter 10 - The Aussie Investor's Toolkit - Shares, ETFs, and Superannuation..................48
Chapter 11 - Property the Right Way - Not Just the "Australian Dream"...........................53
Chapter 12 - Balancing Property and Shares - The Best of Both Worlds...........................57
Chapter 13 - Protecting Your Wealth - Insurance & Estate Planning.................................62
Chapter 14 - The FIRE Path - Financial Independence, Retire Early (Australian Edition)...67
Chapter 15 - Money and Meaning - Building a Life You Love..71
Conclusion - Your Journey Starts Here................75
Appendix - Quick Reference Checklists..............77

About the Author.. 80

Introduction - Why This Book Matters Now

When I was younger, I believed the only way to *get ahead* was to work harder, take on extra shifts, and stash away whatever was left at the end of the week. Like many Australians, I quickly learned that this approach rarely works. Bills pile up, unexpected expenses appear, and no matter how much overtime you put in, the money seems to vanish.

If you've ever felt stuck in that cycle — working hard yet feeling like you're running in place — this book is for you.

Australia today faces a unique financial climate. Wages haven't kept up with inflation, property prices have skyrocketed, and everyday essentials feel more expensive than ever. At the same time, opportunities to grow wealth — through smart saving, investing, and understanding debt — have never been more accessible. The challenge is knowing where to start and how to navigate the rules that are specific to Australian households.

That's why I wrote *Money Made Simple*. This isn't a textbook full of jargon, and it isn't a "get rich quick" scheme. It's a practical guide to help ordinary Australians take control of their finances. Whether you're 18 and just starting out, 40 and worried you've left it too late, or somewhere in between, the principles in this book can help you save, budget, repay debt, and invest wisely.

We'll cover the basics — like setting up a budget that works — and move on to more advanced strategies, including building an emergency fund, understanding the difference between good debt and bad debt, and investing in property and ETFs within the Australian legal framework.

Most importantly, you'll learn how to apply these principles in real life, with examples, numbers, and stories from Australians just like you.

By the end of this book, you won't just know *what* to do — you'll know *how* to do it, step by step. You'll have the tools to break the cycle of financial stress and build a future where money works for you, not against you.

So let's get started. Your journey to financial freedom begins here.

Chapter 1 - The Aussie Money Trap - And How to Escape It

If you've ever wondered why you work hard, earn decent money, yet never seem to get ahead, you're not alone. In Australia, a country with one of the highest standards of living in the world, a surprising number of people live week-to-week. The problem isn't always how much you earn — it's how you think about money.

The Illusion of Comfort

Meet Sarah and Dave — a couple from Adelaide in their mid-thirties. They each earn around $80,000 a year. On paper, that's a healthy household income. But between their mortgage, two car loans, Afterpay installments, weekend brunches, gym memberships, streaming services, and the occasional Bali holiday, their bank balance is always running on fumes.

They're not reckless. They're doing what most Aussies do: living the "good life" now and figuring the rest out later. The problem? Later often arrives sooner than expected — in the form of job loss, medical bills, or interest rate hikes.

This is what I call The Aussie Money Trap:

> *A cycle where lifestyle spending grows with your income, leaving you asset-rich (maybe)*

but cash-poor, and vulnerable to even the smallest financial shock.

Why It's So Common in Australia

1. Easy Credit – Banks will happily give you a credit card limit equal to a month's salary — or more. Buy now, pay… eventually.

2. Cultural Normalisation of Debt – We joke about our HECS-HELP loans and 30-year mortgages like they're badges of honour.

3. Lifestyle Inflation – Every pay rise is followed by a new expense: better car, bigger house, fancier holidays.

4. The 'She'll Be Right' Attitude – Many Australians rely on optimism instead of a plan. Superannuation? "It'll sort itself out."

The First Step to Escaping

The good news? Escaping the trap isn't about giving up everything you enjoy. It's about flipping your financial priorities.

Most people follow this order:
```
Earn → Spend → Save
```

But the wealthy flip it:

`Earn → Save/Invest → Spend what's Left`

By paying yourself first — even if it's just $50 a week to start — you begin to build a buffer. That buffer grows into an emergency fund, then into investments, then into freedom.

The Mindset Shift

To break free, you need to see money not as something that comes in and goes out, but as a tool. A tool for security, opportunity, and choice.

Here are three mindset changes to start with:

1. **Stop Thinking in Weeks** – Weekly pay cycles trick you into short-term thinking. Start thinking in years and decades.

2. **Value Time Over Things** – That $500 on the latest phone upgrade could be two months closer to financial independence.

3. **Accept That Future You Deserves More** – Spending less now isn't punishment — it's an investment in a life you control.

Quick Win Actions (Do This Today)

- Open a High-Interest Online Savings Account – ING, ubank, or similar. This will be your emergency buffer.

- Automate $50/week into it — Non-negotiable.

- Track your spending for 7 days — You'll be shocked where your money actually goes.

- Cancel one unused subscription — Redirect that money to savings.

Key Takeaway: Escaping the Aussie Money Trap starts with changing your order of operations and treating savings like your first bill, not your last. The rest of this book will give you the tools to grow those savings into a life you actually own — not one owned by the bank.

Chapter 2 - The Real Cost of a Latte - Understanding Your Spending

It's 8:05 a.m. on a Monday in Melbourne.
Ben, a 29-year-old marketing manager, is running late for work. He swings by his favourite cafe, orders a large flat white ($5.50) and a toasted ham-and-cheese croissant ($8). He taps his card without a second thought, rushing to the office with breakfast in hand.

He does this most weekdays. It's his "little treat" — a reward for facing the traffic and another long day. Seems harmless, right? Just a coffee and a snack.

But here's the thing: what feels like nothing in the moment can quietly become thousands of dollars slipping through your fingers every year.

The Latte Factor

The "*latte factor*" is a term popularised by American financial writer David Bach, but it's just as real here in Australia. It refers to those small, regular expenses that don't seem like much individually but add up to serious money over time.

Let's run Ben's numbers:

- Coffee: $5.50
- Croissant: $8.00
- Total per weekday: $13.50
- Times 5 days: $67.50/week
- Times 52 weeks: $3,510/year

That's *just* from his breakfast habit. And it doesn't include Friday night drinks, Uber Eats orders, or the three streaming services he never uses.

The "If You Invested It" Reality

Now, imagine Ben decided to cut that habit in half — bringing breakfast from home 3 days a week and still treating himself twice. He'd save about $2,100/year.

If he invested that $2,100 every year in a low-cost Aussie ETF returning 7% annually, here's what happens:

- After 10 years: $29,133
- After 20 years: $87,146

- After 30 years: $208,495

All from skipping a few cafe visits each week. That's a house deposit in some regional areas — or a serious boost to a super fund.

Why We Overspend Without Noticing

1. **Tap-and-Go Blindness** – We don't "feel" the money leaving.

2. **Small Amount Justification** – "It's only five bucks."

3. **Habit Loops** – We link purchases to routines (morning coffee, lunch break scroll).

How to Spot Your Latte Factor

Everyone's "latte" is different. For some it's takeaway lunch, for others it's online shopping or premium app subscriptions.

Do this now:

1. Track every dollar for 7 days – Use your banking app, or free tools like Frollo or Pocketbook.

2. Highlight anything under $20 you buy regularly.

3. Add up how much that habit costs per year.

4. Ask yourself: *If I cut this in half, where could the money go instead?*

Quick Wins

- **Meal Prep Lite** – You don't have to cook every meal. Even replacing 2 takeaway lunches a week with homemade ones saves $20–$30.

- **Subscription Audit** – Cancel one unused service today.

- **Cash Challenge** – Withdraw $100 cash at the start of the week and use that for all "fun" spending. When it's gone, it's gone.

Key Takeaway: It's not about never having a coffee again — it's about being intentional. Every dollar you save and invest today buys you more freedom tomorrow.

Chapter 3 - Building Your Money Map - The 3-Account System

When most Australians get paid, the money lands in one account — and from there it's a free-for-all. Bills, groceries, rent or mortgage, Friday night takeaway, new sneakers, and that impulse Bunnings trip… all get mixed in together.

The problem? When everything's in one bucket, you can't tell if you're winning or falling behind. And often, you don't notice you're in trouble until the card declines.

The solution is to build a **Money Map** — a simple, automated system that directs your income to the right places before you have a chance to spend it on the wrong ones.

Why a Money Map Works

Think of it like plumbing. If water flows into one big tank with no pipes or valves, it will spill out wherever there's an opening. But if you install pipes to channel that water into separate tanks — one for drinking, one for the garden, one for emergencies — you're in control of where every drop goes.

Your income works the same way. You need dedicated "*tanks*" (bank accounts) for each purpose.

The 3-Account System

This is a bare-bones version that works for almost everyone, whether you're earning $45k or $145k a year.

1. **Everyday Account – Living Expenses**

    - **Purpose:** Cover your regular bills and day-to-day spending.

    - **Examples:** Rent/mortgage, utilities, groceries, transport.

    - **Tip:** Use a low-fee transaction account with a debit card.

2. **Savings & Safety Account – Emergency Fund**

    - **Purpose:** Your financial safety net.

    - **Target:** 3–6 months' worth of living expenses.

    - **Tip:** Keep this in a separate high-interest online savings account (ING, ubank, AMP Saver).

    - **Rule:** No touching unless it's a genuine emergency (job loss, medical, urgent repairs).

3. **Future Wealth Account – Investing & Growth**

    - **Purpose:** Build wealth through ETFs, property deposits, super top-ups, or other investments.

    - **Tip:** This account should be with a bank or brokerage separate from your main everyday bank so it's less tempting to dip into.

How to Set It Up

1. **Pick Your Accounts** – If possible, choose banks with good app controls and no monthly fees.

2. **Set Automatic Transfers** – On payday, transfer a fixed percentage to each account. For example:

    - `60% → Everyday Account`

    - `20% → Savings & Safety Account`

- 20% → Future Wealth Account Adjust the ratios to suit your goals — debt repayment may take a higher share early on.

3. **Name Your Accounts** – Literally label them in your banking app: *Bills*, *Emergency Fund*, *Freedom Fund*. It makes spending from them feel more intentional.

Aussie Example: Jess' Transformation

Jess, a nurse from Brisbane, was earning $78,000 but had just $900 in savings. After setting up the 3-Account System and automating transfers, she built a $15,000 emergency fund in 18 months and started investing $250/month into an ETF. She didn't earn more — she just redirected what she already had.

Pro Tip: Link It to an Offset Account

If you own a home with a mortgage, your *Savings and Safety Account* could be an offset account. This reduces your loan interest while keeping your emergency cash accessible.

Key Takeaway: Your Money Map removes willpower from the equation. By automating where your money goes the moment it arrives, you ensure your savings and investments happen *first* — and your lifestyle fits around them, not the other way around.

Chapter 4 - The Bare-Bones Budget - Spending Only on What Matters

If you've ever tried to follow a complicated spreadsheet budget only to abandon it after two weeks, you're not alone.
Most budgets fail for **one** simple reason: they're too detailed to live with. Tracking every coffee, every parking meter, every $2 coin — it's exhausting.

A better approach is what I call the Bare-Bones Budget: a simple, flexible plan that covers the essentials, gives you freedom for the fun stuff, and still keeps you on track to build wealth.

Why "Bare-Bones" Works

In tough times — job loss, medical bills, interest rate hikes — knowing your bare-bones budget is a lifesaver. It's the minimum amount you need to keep your life running without going into debt.

But here's the secret: even in good times, living *close* to your bare-bones number lets you save and invest far more than most people without feeling deprived.

Step 1 – Find Your Bare-Bones Number

Your bare-bones number is made up of *non-negotiable* expenses — the ones that keep the lights on and food on the table.

Typical categories:

- Housing (rent/mortgage)
- Utilities (electricity, gas, water)
- Groceries
- Transport (fuel, public transport, car rego/insurance)
- Insurance (home, contents, health, income protection)
- Minimum debt repayments

Example:

Expense	Monthly Cost
Mortgage	$2,100
Utilities	$250
Groceries	$800
Transport	$300
Insurance	$200
Debt repayments	$300
Total Bare-Bones:	$3,950/month

This is the number that keeps you afloat.

Step 2 – Add the Fun Money

Life isn't meant to be lived on bare-bones forever.

Once your essentials are covered, add a *controlled* amount for discretionary spending — dining out, streaming, hobbies, travel.

Scott Pape (The Barefoot Investor) uses a "splurge" account for this. I like to set it as a fixed weekly amount. That way, you can enjoy guilt-free spending *within* limits.

Step 3 – Use the 60/20/20 Rule (Australian Style)

A simple budget breakdown for most households:

- 60% Needs – your bare-bones essentials

- 20% Savings/Investments – goes straight to your Savings & Safety + Future Wealth Accounts

- 20% Wants – guilt-free fun

If you're in heavy debt repayment mode, you might temporarily shift to 70/20/10 until debts are cleared.

Step 4 – Automate It

- Direct deposit your pay into your Everyday Account.

- Set automatic transfers to Savings & Safety and Future Wealth Accounts on payday.

- Leave your discretionary "fun" money in your Everyday Account — but withdraw cash for it if you tend to overspend.

Case Study: Michael's Mortgage Smash

Michael, a teacher from Perth, cut his "wants" budget from 20% to 10% for two years, funnelling the extra 10% into his mortgage offset account. Result? He shaved five years off his loan term and saved over $65,000 in interest.

Key Takeaway: A Bare-Bones Budget isn't about living miserably. It's about knowing your minimum needs, automating your savings, and making every extra dollar work towards your freedom — instead of vanishing into random spending.

Chapter 5 - Automate to Dominate - Setting Your Finances on Autopilot

If you've ever missed a bill, forgotten to transfer savings, or spent your "extra" money on a weekend splurge, you've experienced the danger of relying on memory and willpower to manage your finances.

The truth is, even the most disciplined people are human. Life gets busy. We forget.

That's why *automation* is your secret weapon — it turns good financial habits into something that happens without you thinking about it.

Why Automation Works

1. **No Temptation** – If the money's already gone to savings or investments before you see it, you can't spend it.

2. **No Late Fees** – Bills are paid on time, every time.

3. **Consistency** – Wealth is built through small, repeated actions — not one-off efforts.

Think of automation as a "financial conveyor belt." Your money comes in at one end, gets sorted into the right places, and you only touch what's left for day-to-day spending.

The Aussie Payday Automation Flow

Let's say you get paid on Thursdays. Here's what happens every payday without you lifting a finger:

1. Income lands in your Everyday Account

2. Automatic transfer to Savings & Safety Account (e.g., 15% of pay)

3. Automatic transfer to Future Wealth Account (e.g., 15% of pay)

4. Direct debit for recurring bills (utilities, phone, insurance) from Everyday Account

5. What's left is your spending money until the next payday

Setting It Up Step-by-Step

1. **Choose Your Transfer Days** – Ideally, the day you're paid so the money moves before you can spend it.

2. **Log into Online Banking** – Set recurring transfers for your savings and investments.

3. **Set Up Direct Debits** – For fixed bills like rent/mortgage, utilities, loan repayments.

4. **Link Your Fun Money Card** – Only use this for discretionary spending.

5. **Review Quarterly** – Check if you can increase your automated savings rate after pay rises or debt repayments.

Extra Aussie Tips for Automation

- Use Offset Accounts for Savings – If you have a mortgage, keeping savings in an offset account can reduce interest and speed up your payoff.

- Salary Sacrifice into Super – Ask your employer to send extra into your superannuation before tax — it reduces taxable income and boosts retirement savings.

- Round-Ups – Banks like CommBank and ING let you round up every purchase to the nearest dollar and put the spare change into savings or investments.

Case Study: Lisa's Invisible Wealth

Lisa, a 34-year-old from Sydney, automated $300/month into a Vanguard ETF in 2015. She barely noticed it leaving her account. By 2025, without any extra effort, she had over $50,000 invested — simply because she set it and forgot it.

Key Takeaway: Automation removes the decision-making and discipline from managing money. Once it's set up, wealth building becomes effortless — and you're no longer relying on "trying to remember" to do the right thing.

Chapter 6 - The Emergency Fund - Your First Financial Safety Net

Imagine your car breaks down, your washing machine floods the laundry, or you get a call that your job is being made redundant.

For many Australians, the immediate reaction isn't "No problem, I've got this covered."

It's panic — followed by reaching for a credit card or taking out a personal loan.

An emergency fund is your antidote to that panic. It's a financial buffer that protects you from life's inevitable surprises — without sending you into debt.

Why You Need One

- **Avoid Debt Spiral** – Without a buffer, emergencies get funded on credit, which leads to interest payments, which eat into your future income.

- **Peace of Mind** – You sleep better knowing you could survive a job loss or major expense.

- **Financial Freedom Accelerator** – An emergency fund lets you invest without fear of having to sell during a market dip.

How Much Should You Have?

The classic advice is 3–6 months of living expenses.

In Australia, that means your bare-bones budget from **Chapter 4** multiplied by 3–6.

Example:
If your bare-bones budget is $4,000/month:

- 3 months = $12,000

- 6 months = $24,000

Start with a mini goal of $2,000 — enough to cover most small emergencies — then build up from there.

Where to Keep It

- **High-Interest Online Savings Account** – ING, ubank, AMP Saver, or similar.

- **Offset Account** – If you have a mortgage, parking your emergency fund here can save you interest while keeping cash available.

- **Not in Investments** – Shares and ETFs can drop in value right when you need the money. Keep this fund safe and liquid.

How to Build It Fast

1. **Automate Transfers** – Even $50/week adds up.

2. **Redirect Windfalls** – Tax refunds, bonuses, side hustle income.

3. **Cut & Redirect** – Cancel unused subscriptions, pause non-essential upgrades, and funnel that cash into your emergency fund.

4. **Use a Separate Bank** – Keeping it at a different bank makes it less tempting to dip into.

Case Study: Tom's Lifesaver

Tom, a tradesman from Adelaide, built a $10,000 emergency fund over two years. When he injured his back and couldn't work for six weeks, his income protection insurance didn't kick in immediately. That emergency fund covered his mortgage, bills, and groceries — without touching a credit card.

Quick Aussie Tip

Some people confuse their offset account with an emergency fund.

It can be both — but only if you have the discipline not to dip into it for non-emergencies. Label it in your online banking as "Emergency Fund" to remind yourself.

Key Takeaway: Your emergency fund is the foundation of financial freedom. Before you think about paying off extra debt or investing heavily, make sure you've got your safety net in place — because building wealth means nothing if one crisis wipes it all out.

The next natural step after protecting yourself is tackling the biggest drag on wealth building — bad debt. That brings us to Chapter 7 – The Debt Detox – Breaking Bad Money Habits, where we'll create a realistic, step-by-step plan for clearing consumer debt fast in Australia.

Chapter 7 - The Debt Detox
Breaking Bad Money Habits

Debt can be a useful tool — but only when it's used strategically (we'll cover *good* debt in Chapter 8).

For most people though, debt is a silent thief, taking tomorrow's income to pay for yesterday's spending.

And in Australia, it's easy to fall into the trap. Credit card offers, buy-now-pay-later services, and "interest-free" store finance are everywhere. But the truth is simple: if you're paying double-digit interest, you're working for the bank, not yourself.

The Real Cost of Bad Debt

Meet Emily, a 32-year-old from Perth. She owes:

- $6,000 on a credit card at 19.94% interest

- $3,000 on Afterpay and Zip Pay combined

- $7,500 personal loan at 12% interest

Her minimum repayments total $550/month. But because of the high interest, she's barely scratching the surface of the balances.

If Emily only pays the minimum on her credit card, that $6,000 will take over 25 years to clear and cost her more than $14,000 in interest alone.

Step 1 – Stop Adding to the Debt

This means:

- Stop using credit cards (switch to debit).

- Delete buy-now-pay-later apps.

- Pause any new discretionary spending until you have a plan in place.

Step 2 – List All Debts

Write down:

1. Lender or service

2. Balance owing

3. Interest rate

4. Minimum repayment

This will show you exactly what you're up against.

Step 3 – Pick Your Payoff Strategy

Option 1: Debt Snowball – Pay off the smallest debt first, then roll its payment into the next one.

- *Pros*: Quick wins, builds momentum.

- *Best for*: People who need motivation to stay consistent.

Option 2: Debt Avalanche – Pay off the debt with the highest interest rate first, then move to the next.

- *Pros*: Saves the most money in interest.

- *Best for*: People motivated by numbers.

Step 4 – Find Extra Repayment Money

- Use savings from your Bare-Bones Budget.

- Sell unused items.

- Take a short-term side hustle.

- Direct tax refunds straight to debt.

Step 5 – Renegotiate Where You Can

- Call your credit card provider and ask for a lower interest rate.

- Consider a 0% balance transfer credit card (but only if you cut up the old card and commit to paying it off within the interest-free period).

- For personal loans, ask your lender about early repayment without penalties.

Case Study: Matt's $20k Turnaround

Matt from Melbourne had $20,000 spread across credit cards and store finance. By using the avalanche method, consolidating some debt to a lower interest rate, and throwing every spare dollar at the highest-interest card, he cleared all debt in 22 months — saving over $6,000 in interest.

Avoiding the Relapse

- Keep just one debit card linked to your Everyday Account.

- Use your emergency fund instead of credit when life happens.

- Keep tracking spending for at least 3 months after becoming debt-free to avoid old habits creeping back.

Key Takeaway: Paying off bad debt isn't just about freeing up money — it's about reclaiming your future income and breaking the cycle of borrowing from tomorrow to fund today.

Next, we'll move from clearing bad debt to understanding how to use good debt strategically. In Chapter 8 – Good Debt vs. Bad Debt – The Australian Perspective, we'll cover how to spot the difference, when borrowing can make you wealthier, and when it's a trap.

Chapter 8 - Good Debt vs. Bad Debt - The Australian Perspective

Not all debt is created equal.

Some debt drains your finances and keeps you stuck in the past. Other debt — used strategically — can help you buy assets that grow in value and create income.

The key is knowing the difference.

What is Bad Debt?

Bad debt is money you borrow to buy things that:

1. Lose value quickly, and

2. Don't generate income.

Examples in Australia:

- Credit cards for clothes, gadgets, or holidays

- Buy Now, Pay Later for furniture or electronics

- Personal loans for weddings or renovations that don't increase property value

- Car loans for expensive vehicles beyond your needs

Why it's bad: You pay interest on something that's worth less every day, with no return on investment.

What is Good Debt?

Good debt is borrowing to buy something that has the potential to:

1. Increase in value over time, or

2. Generate income that exceeds the debt cost.

Examples in Australia:

- **HECS-HELP loans** – Interest-free (indexed to inflation only), enabling higher earning potential.

- **Investment property loans** – Property can grow in value, generate rental income, and offer tax benefits (negative gearing, depreciation).

- **Business loans** – Funding that enables higher profits over time.

- **Margin loans for shares/ETFs *(high risk)*** – Only if used carefully, as market drops can magnify losses.

How to Tell the Difference

Ask yourself before taking on debt:

1. Will this purchase *make me money* or *lose me money*?

2. Is the return likely to be higher than the interest rate?

3. Is there a safer way to get the same benefit without borrowing?

If the answer to #1 is "lose me money" — it's bad debt. Simple.

The Aussie Tax Advantage of Some Good Debt

In Australia, interest on loans for income-producing assets (like rental properties or certain business loans) can be tax-deductible.
Example:

- If you borrow $500,000 for an investment property at 6% interest, that's $30,000/year in interest.

- If the property is negatively geared, you may be able to deduct part of that from your taxable income — reducing your tax bill.

But beware: tax deductions don't make a bad investment good. The property still needs strong fundamentals (location, rental demand, growth potential).

Case Study: Sarah's Smart vs. Silly Debt

Sarah, from Brisbane, had $8,000 in credit card debt (bad debt) and a $400,000 mortgage on an investment unit (good debt). She paid off the credit card within 12 months using the avalanche method, then redirected the freed-up payments into extra mortgage repayments. Over time, her investment property grew in value by $150,000, while the credit card would have cost her $12,000 in interest if left unpaid.

Key Takeaway: Bad debt keeps you working for the bank. Good debt, when managed wisely, can help the bank work for you. The trick is to use debt only when it buys you an asset that grows or earns — and never confuse a depreciating purchase with an investment.

Next up, we'll zoom in on the single biggest debt most Australians will ever take on — and show you how to pay it off faster. Chapter 9 – Smarter Mortgage Management – Owning Your Home Sooner will cover offset accounts, refinancing, and avoiding mortgage traps.

Chapter 9 - Smarter Mortgage Management - Owning Your Home Sooner

For many Australians, a mortgage is a 25–30 year commitment that quietly drains hundreds of thousands of dollars in interest over its lifetime.

But it doesn't have to be that way.

With a few smart moves, you can cut years off your loan and save a fortune — without living on baked beans.

The True Cost of Your Mortgage

Let's say you buy a home for $650,000 with a 20% deposit ($130,000) and borrow $520,000 at 6% interest over 30 years.

- Monthly repayment: $3,118

- Total interest over the life of the loan: $600,342

Yes — you'd pay more in interest than the original loan unless you take action.

1. Use an Offset Account

An offset account is a bank account linked to your mortgage. The balance in it offsets your loan balance for interest calculations.
Example:

- Loan: $520,000

- Offset balance: $20,000

- Interest charged on: $500,000

Even a small, consistent balance in your offset account can save you thousands over time.

Tip: Keep your emergency fund here if you're disciplined not to touch it for non-emergencies.

2. Make Extra Repayments

Every extra dollar you put on your mortgage saves you interest and shortens the term.

Example:

- Extra $200/month = loan paid off 4 years sooner, saving $78,000 in interest.

- Extra $500/month = loan paid off 8 years sooner, saving $145,000 in interest.

3. Pay Fortnightly Instead of Monthly

Fortnightly repayments mean you make 26 half-payments a year (the equivalent of 13 monthly payments).

This small change alone can knock 2–3 years off your mortgage.

4. Review & Refinance

Don't "set and forget" your loan:

- Check your rate annually.

- If your lender won't match a competitor's lower rate, consider refinancing.

- Watch for fees — sometimes staying with the same bank and negotiating is cheaper than switching.

5. Avoid the Traps

- **Interest-Only Loans on Your Home** – Unless you're using it as a short-term strategy for cash flow, you're just delaying repayment and paying more interest.

- **Redraw Temptation** – Redraw facilities let you take back extra repayments. Good for emergencies, bad if you use it to fund holidays.

Case Study: Karen & Steve's 10-Year Plan

Karen and Steve from Adelaide refinanced their $450,000 mortgage from 6.2% to 5.5% and switched to fortnightly repayments, adding $300/month in extra repayments. Their original 28 years remaining dropped to 18 years, saving them over $140,000 in interest.

Key Takeaway: A mortgage is the biggest debt you'll likely ever take on — and the biggest opportunity to save money if you manage it aggressively. Every extra dollar and every smart strategy chips years off your loan and keeps more money in your pocket.

From here, we'll transition into building wealth beyond your home — starting with shares and ETFs.

In Chapter 10 – The Aussie Investor's Toolkit – Shares, ETFs, and Superannuation, we'll cover how to start investing, avoid common mistakes, and use tax advantages to grow your wealth.

Chapter 10 - The Aussie Investor's Toolkit - Shares, ETFs, and Superannuation

Once you've built an emergency fund and cleared bad debt, the next step is to put your money to work.

In Australia, that usually means three key vehicles: individual shares, exchange-traded funds (ETFs), and superannuation.

Each has its pros, cons, and tax advantages — and knowing how to use them can fast-track your path to financial freedom.

1. Shares

Buying shares means owning a slice of a company. When the company does well, you can benefit in two ways:

- **Capital growth** – the share price goes up.

- **Dividends** – the company pays you a portion of its profits.

Australian advantage:
Dividends from Aussie companies often come with

franking credits, which can reduce your tax bill or even result in a refund if your marginal tax rate is low.

Example:
If you receive $700 in fully franked dividends, you also get a $300 franking credit (representing the tax the company already paid). Your taxable income includes $1,000, but you get that $300 credit to offset your tax bill.

2. ETFs (Exchange-Traded Funds)

An ETF is like a basket of shares that trades on the stock exchange.

Instead of buying individual companies, you buy into a fund that holds dozens or even hundreds of them.

Why they're great for beginners:

- Diversification from day one.

- Low fees compared to managed funds.

- Easy to buy and sell through any online broker.

Popular Aussie ETFs:

- VAS – Tracks the top 300 companies on the ASX.

- VGS – International shares.

- A200 – Tracks the top 200 Aussie companies, with one of the lowest fees in the market.

3. Superannuation

Super is your retirement powerhouse. You might not be able to access it until your preservation age (currently 60 for most people), but the tax benefits make it a must-use tool.

Tax perks:

- Concessional contributions (like employer super + salary sacrifice) are taxed at 15%, which is often much lower than your marginal tax rate.

- Investment earnings inside super are also taxed at a maximum of 15%.

Smart moves:

- Salary sacrifice extra into super if you can.

- Check your investment option – many people leave their super in a default "balanced" fund without realising they could choose growth or index-based options.

How Much to Start Investing?

You don't need thousands to begin.

- Many online brokers (e.g., Pearler, SelfWealth, CMC) let you start with $500 per trade.

- Some micro-investing apps (e.g., Raiz, Spaceship) let you start with as little as $5 — great for building the habit.

Avoiding Common Mistakes

- **Chasing "hot" tips** – By the time you hear it, the market probably already has.

- **Over-trading** – Frequent buying/selling racks up brokerage fees and taxes.

- **No plan** – Investing without a clear strategy is like sailing without a compass.

Case Study: Jack's ETF Snowball

Jack, a 27-year-old from Melbourne, started investing $500/month into VAS and VGS. After 5 years, his portfolio grew to $42,000 — not just from contributions, but from compounding returns. He didn't pick stocks, time the market, or read charts — just invested regularly and left it alone.

Key Takeaway: Shares, ETFs, and superannuation each have unique strengths. Used together, they form a powerful wealth-building trio — giving you diversification, tax advantages, and the potential for strong long-term growth.

Next, we'll dive into Chapter 11 – Property the Right Way – Not Just the "Australian Dream", where we'll break down how to analyse a property deal, avoid overleveraging, and understand tax impacts like CGT and negative gearing.

Chapter 11 - Property the Right Way - Not Just the "Australian Dream"

In Australia, property isn't just a place to live — it's almost a national obsession.

BBQs turn into real estate debates, and auction results make the evening news.

But while property can be a powerful wealth builder, it's also where many Australians overextend themselves financially, relying on hope rather than numbers.

The Myth of "Property Always Goes Up"

Yes, property prices in Australia have generally trended upwards over decades.

But that doesn't mean *every* property is a good investment. Buying the wrong property — in the wrong area, at the wrong price — can lead to years of poor growth, negative cash flow, and high stress.

The Fundamentals of a Good Investment Property

1. **Location with Growth Potential** – Look for population growth, infrastructure investment, and strong local employment.

2. **Rental Demand** – Low vacancy rates (under 3%) mean you're more likely to keep tenants and avoid long gaps without rent.

3. **Cash Flow** – Rental income should cover as much of your costs as possible.

4. **Potential for Capital Growth** – Areas with a history of above-average price growth, not just recent spikes.

The Numbers You Must Know

Before you buy, calculate:

- Gross Rental Yield = (Annual Rent ÷ Property Price) × 100
  Example: $500/week rent = $26,000/year. On a $650,000 property:
  $26,000 ÷ $650,000 × 100 = 4% gross yield.

- Net Yield – Gross yield minus expenses (rates, insurance, maintenance, management fees).

- Cash Flow – Your actual out-of-pocket cost after rent, expenses, and loan repayments.

Tax Considerations

- **Negative Gearing** – If rental income is less than your expenses, the loss can be deducted from your taxable income, reducing your tax bill. But remember: a tax deduction is not a profit — you're still losing money overall.

- **Capital Gains Tax (CGT)** – When you sell, any gain is taxed. If you've held the property for more than 12 months, you get a 50% discount on the gain for tax purposes.

- **Depreciation** – You can claim deductions for the wear and tear on the building and some fixtures. A quantity surveyor can prepare a depreciation schedule.

Avoiding Common Traps

- Buying off-the-plan without understanding market risks.

- Ignoring strata fees and special levies in apartments.

- Over-leveraging with multiple properties and no buffer.

- Choosing property purely for tax benefits rather than solid fundamentals.

Case Study: Rachel's Numbers-First Purchase

Rachel from Brisbane was tempted to buy a flashy apartment in the CBD. Instead, she chose a 3-bedroom house in a growing suburb with a new train station being built nearby. It had a 4.8% gross yield, a low vacancy rate, and room for renovation. Five years later, it's worth $180,000 more — and she has positive cash flow.

Key Takeaway: Property can be a wealth-building machine if you buy with your head, not your heart. Focus on growth areas, strong rental demand, and sustainable cash flow — and remember, "the Australian Dream" should be freedom, not a lifetime mortgage.

From here, the next logical step is Chapter 12 – Balancing Property and Shares – The Best of Both Worlds, where we'll compare the strengths and weaknesses of each and show how combining them can create a safer, more resilient wealth plan.

Chapter 12 - Balancing Property and Shares - The Best of Both Worlds

In Australia, people tend to fall into two camps:

1. **The Property-Only Crew** – "Shares are too risky; bricks and mortar are safe."

2. **The Shares-Only Crew** – "Property is slow, expensive, and full of hidden costs."

The truth? Both can build wealth — and both have weaknesses.

A smart investor uses them together, creating a balanced portfolio that can withstand market ups and downs.

The Strengths of Property

- **Leverage** – You can borrow large sums at relatively low interest rates, magnifying returns.

- **Tangible Asset** – You can see it, touch it, and rent it out.

- **Inflation Hedge** – Rents and property values often rise with inflation.

- **Tax Benefits** – Negative gearing, depreciation, CGT discount.

The Weaknesses of Property

- **High Entry Costs** – Deposits, stamp duty, legal fees.

- **Ongoing Expenses** – Maintenance, rates, insurance, management fees.

- **Illiquid** – Selling takes time and can be costly.

- **Market Cycles** – Property values can stagnate for years in some areas.

The Strengths of Shares & ETFs

- **Low Entry Point** – Start with as little as $500.

- **Liquidity** – Buy and sell in seconds.

- **Diversification** – One ETF can give exposure to hundreds of companies.

- **Income + Growth** – Dividends plus capital gains.

The Weaknesses of Shares & ETFs

- **Volatility** – Prices can swing daily.

- **Behaviour Risk** – Many people panic sell during downturns.

- **No Leverage Advantage** – Borrowing to invest in shares (margin loans) carries high risk.

How They Work Together

- **Cash Flow & Growth** – Property may provide leveraged capital growth, while shares offer liquid, dividend-paying investments.

- **Diversification** – If property markets slow, shares might rise — and vice versa.

- **Flexibility** – Shares can be sold in part to fund opportunities, while property anchors your portfolio.

A Simple Balanced Strategy

1. **Build your base** – Emergency fund + super contributions.

2. **First growth phase** – Buy a well-researched investment property with good rental yield and growth potential.

3. **Diversify early** – Start an ETF portfolio alongside the property, even with small amounts.

4. **Long-term balance** – Aim for 50–70% of net worth in property, 30–50% in shares/super — adjusting as you age and risk tolerance changes.

Case Study: Adam & Priya's Dual Engine

Adam and Priya from Sydney bought an investment unit in 2014 and began investing $400/month into ETFs the same year. Over 10 years, their property gained $350,000 in value, while their ETF portfolio grew to $80,000. The property gave them leverage and growth, the shares gave them liquidity and dividends. Together, they created a stable, growing portfolio.

Key Takeaway: You don't have to choose between property and shares. Use each for its strengths, balance the weaknesses, and you'll have a portfolio that's more resilient — and more flexible — than going all-in on one asset class.

From here, we move into the protection phase of wealth with Chapter 13 – Protecting Your Wealth – Insurance & Estate Planning, where we'll cover how to safeguard everything you've built.

Chapter 13 - Protecting Your Wealth - Insurance & Estate Planning

You've worked hard to save, invest, and grow your financial position.

But without the right protection, a single accident, illness, or legal oversight can wipe it all out.

In Australia, too many people overlook this stage — either because it's not "exciting" or they think bad things happen to "other people." The reality? Protection is just as important as growth.

Step 1 – Insurance: Your Financial Safety Net

Insurance isn't about fear — it's about certainty. You're buying peace of mind that no matter what happens, you or your family can cover the bills.

Types to Consider

1. **Income Protection**

    - Replaces part of your income (typically up to 70%) if you can't work due to illness or injury.

- Premiums are tax-deductible if paid outside super.
- Check if you already have cover through your super fund.

2. **Life Insurance**

    - Pays a lump sum to your beneficiaries if you die or are diagnosed with a terminal illness.
    - Covers debts, living expenses, and future costs for your family.

3. **Total & Permanent Disability (TPD) Insurance**

    - Pays a lump sum if you become permanently disabled and can't work.
    - Often bundled with life insurance inside super.

4. **Trauma/Critical Illness Cover**

    - Pays a lump sum if you suffer certain serious medical conditions (e.g., heart attack, cancer, stroke).

- Helps cover medical bills, lifestyle adjustments, or time off work.

5. **General Insurance**

    - Home, contents, car, landlord, and business insurance protect your physical assets.

Step 2 – Estate Planning: Your Final Instructions

Estate planning ensures your wealth goes where you want it to — with minimal delays, disputes, or unnecessary taxes.

Key Documents

1. **Will** – Specifies how your assets are distributed. Without one, state laws decide — and it may not align with your wishes.

2. **Enduring Power of Attorney (EPOA)** – Appoints someone to handle your financial/legal matters if you can't.

3. **Advance Care Directive / Medical Power of Attorney** – Outlines your wishes for medical care if you can't communicate them.

4. **Binding Death Benefit Nomination for Super** – Tells your super fund exactly who should receive your superannuation. Without it, the trustee decides.

Australian Tax Considerations

- Life insurance payouts to *financial dependants* are generally tax-free.

- Superannuation death benefits to *non-dependants* may attract tax.

- Property and investments may trigger capital gains tax upon transfer or sale.

Case Study: The Cost of Not Planning

David, a 45-year-old from Perth, passed away suddenly without a will. His estate took 18 months to settle, during which his partner couldn't access his bank accounts. Had he prepared a will and nominated beneficiaries for his super, the process could have been completed in weeks.

Key Takeaway: Growing wealth is only half the job — protecting it ensures your family, your future, and your legacy are secure. A solid insurance plan and clear estate documents mean you stay in control, even when you're not here to make the decisions.

From here, we move into Chapter 14 – The FIRE Path – Financial Independence, Retire Early (Australian Edition), where we'll cover how to calculate your "freedom number" and create a realistic plan for early retirement in Australia.

Chapter 14 - The FIRE Path - Financial Independence, Retire Early (Australian Edition)

Imagine waking up without an alarm, knowing your bills are covered by passive income.

No boss. No commute. Just the freedom to spend your days how *you* choose.

That's the dream behind FIRE — Financial Independence, Retire Early.

And while it started as a US-based movement, it can absolutely work in Australia — if you understand our tax system, superannuation rules, and living costs.

Step 1 – Know Your Freedom Number

Your Freedom Number is the amount of money you need invested to cover your annual expenses — forever.

A common rule in FIRE is the 4% Rule:

- You can safely withdraw 4% of your investments each year without running out of money.

Example:
If you need $60,000/year:
$60,000 ÷ 0.04 = $1.5 million invested.

Step 2 – Reduce Before You Accumulate

The smaller your living expenses, the smaller your Freedom Number.

- Pay off your mortgage.

- Eliminate bad debt.

- Build efficient spending habits (from Chapters 2–4).

Step 3 – The Australian Investment Mix

FIRE in Australia often uses a combination of:

1. **ETFs/Shares** – For accessible, liquid investments before retirement age.

2. **Investment Property** – For leveraged growth and rental income.

3. **Superannuation** – For long-term, tax-efficient compounding after preservation age.

Step 4 – Plan for the "Gap Years"

If you retire at 50, you might have 10+ years before you can access super.

That means your non-super investments must cover that period.

Example approach:

- Build $500,000 outside super to live on for 10 years.

- Have $1M+ inside super to take over from age 60.

Step 5 – Keep Inflation in Check

Inflation eats into your spending power. In Australia, long-term inflation averages around 2–3% — which means your investments need to outpace it to maintain your lifestyle.

Step 6 – Protect While You Grow

- Keep an emergency fund (Chapter 6).

- Maintain insurance coverage (Chapter 13).

- Avoid risky "get rich quick" schemes — FIRE is about steady, consistent progress.

Case Study: Natalie's CoastFIRE

Natalie, a 40-year-old teacher from Brisbane, didn't want full FIRE yet but wanted more freedom.
She built up $400,000 in ETFs and two investment properties, then reduced her teaching to three days a week. Her investments now cover 50% of her expenses, and her part-time job covers the rest. She plans to fully retire by 55.

Key Takeaway: FIRE isn't about never working again — it's about having the *choice* to work, retire, travel, or start new projects without worrying about money.

In Australia, combining property, shares, and super — with a plan for your "gap years" — makes early financial freedom possible.

From here, we'll finish strong with Chapter 15 – Money and Meaning – Building a Life You Love, where we'll shift from "how to get money" to "what to do with it" so readers stay motivated and purposeful.

Chapter 15 - Money and Meaning - Building a Life You Love

Money is a tool.

It can buy comfort, security, and options — but beyond a certain point, more dollars don't automatically mean more happiness.

In fact, without a clear vision, it's easy to reach your financial goals and still feel restless. That's why the final step in your financial journey is to connect your money to what truly matters to you.

Step 1 – Define Your "Why"

Ask yourself: *Why am I building wealth?*

- Is it to spend more time with family?
- To travel the world?
- To start a business or passion project?
- To give back to your community?

When your goals are linked to meaning, it's easier to stay disciplined through the years it takes to reach them.

Step 2 – Spend on What Matters, Cut the Rest

From Chapter 4, you learned about the Bare-Bones Budget and discretionary spending.

Here, we take it further:

- Spend freely on the things that bring joy and long-term value.

- Ruthlessly cut the things that don't.

This isn't about frugality for its own sake — it's about intentional living.

Step 3 – Create Your "Life Portfolio"

Your financial portfolio is diversified — your life should be too.

Balance time and resources between:

- **Relationships** – Friends, family, community.

- **Growth** – Education, skills, health.

- **Experiences** – Travel, hobbies, challenges.

- **Contribution** – Volunteering, mentoring, philanthropy.

Step 4 – Build Generational Wealth (If You Want)

For some, the ultimate purpose is ensuring children or grandchildren start life on a stronger footing.

- Consider a family trust.

- Teach financial literacy early.

- Pass down not just money, but values around managing it.

Step 5 – Keep Learning, Keep Adapting

The financial world changes — tax laws, markets, technology, and opportunities evolve.

Commit to reviewing your plan annually. Stay curious, keep reading, and keep refining your approach.

Case Study: Michael's "Enough" Moment

Michael, a 55-year-old engineer from Perth, reached his FIRE number and realised he didn't want to stop working entirely. Instead, he shifted to part-time consulting, started mentoring young engineers, and funded scholarships at his old university. His investments give him freedom — but purpose keeps him fulfilled.

Key Takeaway: Financial freedom isn't the finish line — it's the starting point for a life lived on your own terms. Use the tools and strategies in this book not just to escape financial stress, but to create a life rich in time, experiences, relationships, and meaning.

Conclusion - Your Journey Starts Here

By now, you've got the tools to:

- Understand where your money goes and take control of it

- Build safety nets that protect you from financial shocks

- Use debt strategically instead of being trapped by it

- Grow your wealth through property, shares, ETFs, and super

- Plan for the future while living a life you enjoy now

The most important thing to remember is this:

Knowledge is useless without action.

Don't wait until next year, next month, or even next week. **Start today** — even if it's just setting up your first automatic savings transfer or tracking your spending for the next 7 days.

Small steps, taken consistently, compound into life-changing results.

And in a few years, you'll look back and realise that the financial stress you feel today has been replaced by something far more valuable: freedom.

Your journey to financial security — and a life on your terms — **STARTS NOW**.

If you'd like to go deeper and build your money skills step by step, I've created a 12-month program where you'll receive a new budgeting and saving lesson each month. You can find it on Gumroad — simply enter this URL https://thebudgetnest.gumroad.com/l/Budgetnestfullcourseaccess and start your journey today.

Appendix - Quick Reference Checklists

1. The 3-Account System Setup

    - Everyday Account – Bills & spending

    - Savings & Safety Account – Emergency fund

    - Future Wealth Account – Investments

    - Automatic transfers set up on payday

2. Bare-Bones Budget Formula

    - 60% Needs (bare-bones essentials)

    - 20% Savings/Investments

    - 20% Wants (fun money)

3. Emergency Fund Targets

    - Mini goal: $2,000

    - Ideal: 3–6 months' bare-bones expenses

- Store in high-interest savings or offset account

4. Debt Payoff Plan

- List debts (balance, rate, minimum repayment)
- Choose Snowball (smallest debt first) or Avalanche (highest interest first)
- Automate extra repayments
- Avoid adding new debt

5. Property Investment Checklist

- Location with growth potential
- Vacancy rate under 3%
- Gross yield above 4% (ideally higher)
- Solid cash flow and buffer for interest rate rises
- Tax impacts understood (CGT, negative gearing, depreciation)

6. Share & ETF Starter Steps

- Open a brokerage account

- Choose diversified, low-fee ETFs (e.g., VAS, VGS, A200)

- Start with $500 minimum trade or micro-investing app

- Invest regularly and avoid emotional trading

7. Insurance & Estate Plan

- Life insurance

- Income protection

- TPD and trauma cover

- Will & Enduring Power of Attorney

- Binding death benefit nomination for super

About the Author

Mavis Bloom is an Australian writer who learned the hard way how stressful money can be. Through trial, error, and persistence, she built her own system for budgeting, saving, paying off debt, and starting to invest for the future.

This book reflects the lessons she wishes she had known earlier — practical steps that everyday Australians can use to take back control of their finances. Mavis believes you don't need to be a finance expert or earn six figures to get ahead — you just need clear, simple strategies and the confidence to follow them.

www.ingramcontent.com/pod-product-compliance
Lightning Source LLC
Chambersburg PA
CBHW071253070526
44583CB00017B/2449